ARE YOU A CHAMPION 4 CHRIST?

UNDERSTAND AND IDENTIFY THE ATTRIBUTES OF A CHAMPION AND LEARN HOW TO WIN IN LIFE.

CHIP BRIM

insight
PUBLISHING GROUP

Tulsa, Oklahoma

ARE YOU A CHAMPION 4 CHRIST?

Are You a Champion 4 Christ? by Chip Brim
Published by Insight Publishing Group
8801 S. Yale, Suite 410
Tulsa, OK 74137
(918) 493-1718

Unless otherwise indicated, all Scripture quotations are from the *King James Version* of the Bible. Scripture quotations marked AMP are taken from *The Amplified Bible. Old Testament* copyright © 1965, 1987 by Zondervan Corporation, Grand Rapids, Michigan. *New Testament* copyright © 1958, 1987 by The Lockman Foundation, La Habra, California. Used by permission.

Cover design by Randy & Sue Lofland

ISBN 1-932503-10-2
Library of Congress Card Catalog number: 2003113213

Printed in the United States of America

DEDICATION

To a champion Mother.
I want to dedicate this book to
my mom, Billye Brim.
For all those times when I was
embarrassed to be prayed for,
you did it anyway.
Thanks for pleading the
Blood over me, Mom.
Now I do it over my children.
I love you!

CONTENTS

FOREWORD

God's call upon Chip's life is unique and supernatural. As one who has yearned for and taught about "the glorious Church" for years, I am so pleased at how the Lord has put His hand on my son and given him a message for the bringing forth of a champion Body for our champion Head. The revelation the Lord gives Chip blesses and challenges me to aim for higher heights in the last days of our great race.

Chip has settled for nothing less than winning all his life. Now I see that the Lord was fashioning him for an important role in these last days. His supernatural call and the revelation God has given him will inspire you, as it does me, to finish the race as a champion.

I've always known we would be a glorious Church before the Lord's return. How thrilled I am that my own son has been given such an important revelation to the triumphant church.

Billye Brim

FOREWORD
(continued)

Chip teaches and exemplifies championship Christianity. His life and message inspire believers today to rise to their greatest potential in Christ.

Pastor Mark Hankins
Christian Worship Center
Alexandria, Louisiana

This book is a winner! In his new book, *Are You a Champion 4 Christ?*, Chip Brim boldly challenges the reader to "step up to the plate" and be a champion. This book gives a deeper understanding of tough love and championship living. It is full of hidden nuggets and godly wisdom. Chip will inspire you to leap to your feet and overcome the challenges of life as you discover how you can be a champion 4 Christ.

Pastor Larry Ollison, Ph.D.
Walk on the Water Faith Church
Osage Beach, Missouri

CHAPTER 1

Tough Love

I was raised by two very strong Christian parents. They both loved God, and they both loved our family. But other than that, they were exact opposites.

My dad was a Cherokee Indian. He was *extremely* intense about everything he did; especially playing sports. That's probably why he turned out to be a football hero in his hometown. He was highly competitive and *hated* to lose—at anything! (My wife says that about me, too: "You know, you have to win in everything!")

Dad would even turn things like fishing for crappie (one of his favorite pastimes) into a competition. If you and he were on opposite ends of the boat and you started catching all the fish, he'd turn the boat around!

Then there was Mom. A preacher. Loving. Kind. Goody Two-shoes. I don't think she ever sinned a day in her life. You know the type.

My sister Brenda and I played sports in school. You should have heard some of the pep talks we got from these two before our games.

Dad would say, "Get the first lick in!"

But Mom would say, "Now you turn the other cheek, Honey."

Dad would say, "You get on out there and rip their heads off!"

But Mom would say, "Walk in love."

Dad would say, "You let them know who you are!"

But Mom would say, "You let them know who you are in Christ."

I'm telling you, it was something else!

And how did all this affect me as a linebacker on the school football team?

Well, whenever I broke out of our team huddle and set up across from my competition, I'd look him right in the eye and growl, "I'm going to rip your head off—in the Name of Jesus!"

Talk about getting some funny looks from people! You could see it on their faces: *What did he say?* Then the next time the other team broke out of their huddle, I could see them all looking and pointing my way, saying, "That's the guy, right there!"

Oddly enough, this tough-but-tender combination ended up serving me well later on as I matured in my fourteen year coaching career. Things were a little rough in the beginning, however.

Since my first love was football, that's where I started. But even though I was as intense about coaching as I could be, we still weren't very good.

It was a real disappointment, but I didn't have anyone to blame but myself. After all, I didn't bother asking God for His help or guidance. I was too busy trying to figure everything out and handle it all on my own.

It didn't take me long to see that the football thing just wasn't going to work, so I decided to go into baseball instead.

That wasn't much better. In fact, we were a joke. We were so bad that we were the only team to lose three games in a doubleheader. We were so bad that we threw a victory party after a rain-out game. I think we probably still hold part of the record for worsts in a season.

You get the idea. It was pitiful.

And I *hated* it! I *hated* losing—especially considering the way I was raised.

But then God showed me how to succeed in coaching, and things began to turn around for me.

"Lord, Help Me!"

God will actually help you on your job, if you let Him. And eventually I did. The whole situation finally became so frustrating to me that I decided I'd better talk to Him about it.

"God, I don't want to be bad. I like to win. Lord, help me! I want to be one of those guys on TV who says, 'And I give all the glory to God that we won this championship!' God, I want to be that person."

So He helped me. He really did.

He told me that the key to being a successful coach was "tough love."

What's tough love?

Well, there are two parts to it. There's the *tough* part and then there's the *love* part.

The tough part is the part where you teach discipline, respect, responsibility, and obedience. (*Obedience*, by the way, means "to hear intelligently." In other words, you *hear* it and *do* it the first time.)

"You're doing the tough part," the Lord told me.

And I was. I was fresh out of college sports, where I had to run all those laps and do all those push-ups—and I was ready to tell somebody *else* to do that! I definitely had the tough part down!

"Now you need to love them," He said.

"Lord! Love them? Love those stinky, pimply-faced teenage boys? Love them?"

"Yes, love them. Love them, and then watch what happens. Use the same kind of love that you were raised with, the love your parents used with you."

I knew exactly what He was talking about then. My parents were firm with me when I was growing up. I was taught discipline. I was taught respect. I was taught to be responsible. I was taught to obey. But I was *definitely* loved—and I *knew* I was loved—and that made all the difference.

That's the kind of love we need in our homes. That's the kind of love we need in our schools. That's the kind of love we need in our churches. That's the kind of love that breeds champions. Tough love. God's love.

I proved this over and over again in my coaching career once the Lord showed me this principle.

Sometimes there were days when I had to really discipline some players on the field during practice. But after practice, I made sure I let them know I loved them.

I'd say something like, "Hey, you know what? I got on you pretty hard today, didn't I? But do you know why I did that? I did it because I love you. I care about what happens to you."

They couldn't believe it. "Whoa, Coach! What are you talking about? Aren't you mad at me?"

"No, I'm not mad at you. I love you. I care about you. I know you've got a lot of potential, and I just want to see you be the best you can be."

You see, players—like most people—tend to take a lot of things personally that they shouldn't. (That's one of the ways the devil tries to harass us and make us feel inferior.) The way you deal with that is to continually reassure them of your love and support. You love them and love them and love them and love them. Not just on their good days. Not just when they're doing everything right. All the time.

Nothing impacts people like that kind of love. That's the kind of love that changes lives.

A Case in Point

There was one young man in particular who comes to mind. He was a state-champion wrestler and was probably the toughest kid in school. But he had a terrible home life. His dad had left the family, and his mom had a lot of problems of her own. As a result, this guy had absolutely no discipline or direction in his life.

So I started working on him with this tough love. I'd say things like, "I'm going to be your dad. I'm going to teach you what you need to learn."

But he just couldn't understand. So we went round and round on a few things before he got it.

I remember one time when I benched him seven games in a row for having a bad attitude. He'd go on out to his position at third base for pregame warm-up as usual. I'd hit him a ball, and if he did something wrong, I'd get on him a little.

"That's not the way to do it. I know you can do it a little better than that."

"Blankety, blankety, blankety, blank!" he'd grumble back at me.

So I'd tell him to go sit down. Then I'd go over to the press box and tell them I was making a change in the lineup, and he sat out the entire game.

Afterwards, I'd tell him, "I'm doing this because I love you. I care about you."

But he didn't get it. He didn't understand.

That happened seven games in a row.

On the eighth game, we were playing a team that was on a winning streak that was setting a national record. My assistant coaches came up to me and said, "Coach, could you please *not* do that to him today? We need him. You know what kind of a team we're up against here."

"No, I have to teach him," I said.

You could see them all go back to the dug-out, shaking their heads. They just knew it was going to happen again. Everyone on the team knew it was going to happen again.

So there we were at pregame warm-up. Everyone was watching. I hit him a ball—and he fielded it perfectly. Threw it over to first base—perfect!

Then he looked at me.

"You think that's pretty good, don't you?" I said.

He didn't say anything. He just bit his lip and kind of swiped the dirt.

Then as I got ready to hit the ball to the next guy, I told him, "That's what I'm talking about. Great job!"

He hit four for four that game. Did an *outstanding* job at the plate. In fact, his contribution helped us beat that team and break their winning streak.

After the game was over, he asked me to come out to right field with him, so I went. The lights were off and it was just the two of us out there.

"What's up?" I asked him.

He hugged me and started crying. (You've got to remember that this is one of the toughest kids I've ever coached.) Soon I was crying, too!

"I realize now what you're doing, Coach. I realize what you're teaching me. You really love me, and you're teaching me this respect and this discipline because you love me. I see it now."

"Yeah," I told him, "it's all about that. It's not about baseball. Baseball will be over one day. I want you to be a great man."

It was quite a moment. Very moving. Very touching.

This young man went on to make All-State—the best third baseman in Oklahoma. He received a full college scholarship, got his degree, and is now a successful businessman with a wonderful family.

That didn't happen because of me. That happened because of God and His tough love.

"How Do You Do That?"

Because my guys knew I loved them and cared about them, it really wasn't a problem getting maximum effort out of them. They always gave it everything they had—and it was obvious to everyone. Other coaches were constantly asking me, "How do you get your kids to do what they do for you?"

One guy even interrupted me at a coaching clinic to ask me that. (God taught me so much about training champions that I started receiving invitations to hold clinics all over the place on how to have a winning team.)

At one point in this particular clinic, I happened to be drawing out a practice schedule. This man stood right up and bellowed, "We don't care about that! We don't care about your practice schedule!"

All of a sudden it got real quiet, and everybody turned to look at him.

"Okay. What do you want to know?" I asked.

"We've all watched you and your teams. Your guys will literally run through a brick wall for you! Your kids even slide into first base head first! Do you teach that?"

"No, I don't," I told him. "As a matter of fact, it's dangerous. I've tried to stop them, but I can't."

"I've been coaching for thirty years, and my guys hate me. They hate me every year that I coach. How do you do that?"

"Do you really want to know?"

Then I told them all about tough love. I told them what God showed me, how He had blessed me, and how they could apply it. It was a great chance to witness and give glory to God.

But most of them didn't get it. I could tell.

"Love? No way! This is *my* program. I'm not doing that. They either play hard, or they get out."

They wouldn't do it.

But I had already made up *my* mind to do things God's way. And the more I began applying this tough love that He showed me, the more my coaching career began to take off.

- I went to Northwest Missouri State for my master's degree and met my beautiful wife, Candace, in the process.

- From there, I had the opportunity to coach the Hogs in baseball at the University of Arkansas.

- After that, I scouted for the Houston Astros for about four years.

- Then I had the privilege of coaching semi-professional baseball for a while.

I had opportunities at every level—high school, college, semiprofessional, professional—and God blessed me everywhere I went.

During this time, I received a number of honors, won a number of state championships, and had a number of kids go on to play college and professional ball. It was an amazing time in my life. I loved it! And I was careful to give God the glory for all of it—on TV, on radio, in the newspapers, and anywhere else I had the chance to talk about it.

But God had something else in mind. A major change was just around the corner.

CHAPTER 2

The Turning Point

During those years of my life, baseball came first. *My* plan, not God's.

It wasn't that I was running from God, or that I had backslidden. I loved Him and gave Him the glory for everything He had blessed me with. I gave Him glory at every practice, and I gave Him glory every time we took the field. I prayed over my team, and I prayed over my boys individually. God was definitely an important part of my life. I just wasn't putting Him first.

Because He loved me, God still blessed and prospered me as much as He could, and I enjoyed a great deal of success.

But all of that was second best. God had something much greater in store for me.

Two Questions

God knew I needed a change. So one day when I was watching a ball game on TV after church, He asked me two questions.

When the Lord asks you a question, you can count on two things. First, that your life is never going to be the same. And, second, that the answer is probably not going to be a simple yes or no.

His first question was, "Are you as disciplined to Me as your players are to you?"

Wow! I had to think about that.

My players were *very* disciplined. They would do *anything* for me. If I called them up at 2 o'clock in the morning and told them to go down to the stadium and run one hundred laps, they'd say, "Yes sir, Coach!" No whining. No complaining. They'd just do it.

Why?

Because they trusted me, and they craved the championship. They were willing to do whatever it took to win. And if that meant running one hundred laps at 2 o'clock in the morning, then so be it. Let's get after it!

So when the Lord asked me if I was that disciplined to Him, it took me back a little. It was tough to answer.

Don't get me wrong. As I said earlier, it wasn't that I was backslidden. My family was at church every time the doors were open. We were paying our tithes. I was even reading my Bible every night before I went to bed.

But then it dawned on me: I was just a regular, plain ol' Christian.

Now I could see where the Lord was going with this. Being a regular, plain ol' Christian wasn't enough. He wanted me to be a *champion* Christian for Him, just like my players were champion baseball players for me.

Just going to church every time the doors were open didn't qualify me to be a champion. Paying my tithes and reading my Bible didn't qualify me to be a champion either. Something was missing.

Champions crave the championship more than any other team. They make it their number one priority. And they do all the little necessary extra things with their whole heart. That's why they receive the rewards.

While I was thinking about that, the Lord asked me the second question: "Are you seeking Me?"

That was an easy one.

"Of course I'm seeking You, Lord! I go to church every Sunday morning and every Sunday night. I try to make as many Wednesday night services as possible. I teach chapel any time we have a game on Sunday and I have to miss church. My wife teaches Sunday School. We pay our tithes. I read my Bible every night."

Then He asked me again, "Are you seeking Me?"

Now He had me thinking about it. Maybe the answer wasn't a simple yes or no.

I decided to ask my wife about it. "Honey, do you think we're seeking God?"

She thought about it for a while and then gave the same answer that I had given.

Whew! That relieved some of the pressure.

"Why are you asking?" she wanted to know.

"Well, because the Lord keeps asking me if I'm seeking Him," I replied.

"You'd better check into it, then, because the Lord is always right," she cautioned me.

Here came that pressure again!

It wasn't ten minutes later until the Lord asked me again, "Are you seeking Me?"

"Evidently not," I answered, somewhat frustrated.

It was becoming obvious that I really didn't have a revelation of the word *seek*. So I studied it out and discovered that it actually means "crave."

In other words, what the Lord was really asking me was, "Are you *craving* Me?"

Right away, a couple of Bible verses came to mind that had the word *seek* in them:

> But *seek* ye first the kingdom of God, and his righteousness; and all these things shall be added unto you.
>
> MATTHEW 6:33

> But without faith it is impossible to please him: for he that cometh to God must believe that he is, and that he is a rewarder of them that diligently *seek* him.
>
> HEBREWS 11:6

Then I saw it. These two verses go together! If we *seek* Him first—*crave* Him first—and do it diligently, all things and rewards will be added to us.

What things and rewards are we talking about? Well, if we back up a few verses in Matthew 6, we see that Jesus has been talking about physical things like food and clothing. And although Hebrews 11 doesn't mention anything specifically, we know from other passages in the

Bible that there are all kinds of benefits to following God:

> Blessed be the Lord, who daily loadeth us with benefits, even the God of our salvation.
>
> PSALM 68:19

> Bless the Lord, O my soul: and all that is within me, bless his holy name. Bless the Lord, O my soul, and forget not all his benefits: Who forgiveth all thine iniquities; who healeth all thy diseases; Who redeemeth thy life from destruction; who crowneth thee with lovingkindness and tender mercies; Who satisfieth thy mouth with good things; so that thy youth is renewed like the eagle's.
>
> PSALM 103:1-5

God is so good! He has made every possible blessing available to us. But these things come as a result of *seeking* Him—*craving* Him—not just because we are born again.

Don't misunderstand. God *loves* everybody, and His love is unconditional. There's nothing you can do to earn it, and there's nothing you can do to make Him stop.

But His blessings *are* conditional. They are reserved for those who *seek* Him.

Look at Matthew 6:33 and Hebrews 11:6 again. It doesn't say anything there about just standing around and confessing the Word all day while you wait for the blessings to fall on you. (A lot of people do that and then wonder why God didn't show up for them.)

Again, don't misunderstand. God will bless us as much as possible wherever we're at, because He's good and because He loves us. But we'll never experience the *fullness* of His blessings until we *do* what He tells us to do in these verses. We can't just be *hearers* of the Word. We have to be *doers*. We have to *seek* Him. We have to *crave* Him.

And keep in mind here that we're seeking *God*, not His blessings. Seeking Him just for Who He is, not for what He can do for us. Seeking Him just because we love Him, not because we have a problem we want Him to fix.

When we start craving Him like that, the blessings in Matthew 6:33 and Hebrews 11:6 will start running us down and overtaking us!

Craving Him

It didn't take long for me to see that I needed to make some changes. Sure, I loved God, but *crave* Him? I knew I wasn't doing that.

27

Think about it for a moment. Did you ever really *crave* something? I know I can get a witness from some pregnant women on this, but all of us have probably craved something at some point in our lives.

When you crave something, you'll do almost anything you can to get it. And if you don't get it, you're really disappointed. It's a big letdown.

Take Olympic athletes, for example. They work their entire lifetime for that gold medal. They *crave* it! They work eight to ten hours a day at it, and they don't let anything else get in their way. And if they end up in second place, they aren't happy.

You will never hear an interview like this:

"Wow! That was awesome! You blew away the competition! You set all the records! How did you do it?"

"Well, you know, I worked out for about an hour every Sunday morning. Sometimes I slept through it, but at least I showed up. And I'll tell you this, too, boys and girls: Working out on Wednesday nights once in awhile can help, too."

No way!

They'll tell you that they were up before anyone else. They'll tell you that they worked at it when they didn't feel like working at it. They paid the price. They did whatever they had to do to make it happen.

Why?

Because they wanted to be a champion. They craved it more than anything else in their life.

Now let's shift that over to God. Are we really *craving* Him like that right now? I'm not talking about spending eight to ten hours a day reading the Bible. I'm talking about having that hunger, that burning desire, for Him. Are we thinking about Him day and night? Are we craving Him to the point that we'll be disappointed and let down if we're not able to spend time with Him?

I knew that I wasn't, but I wanted to. I wanted His will for me. I wanted to walk in close fellowship with Him. I wanted to hear His voice and be led by Him. Daily. Every step of the way.

But the first thing that came to my mind was, *I don't have time.*

"Lord, I can't think of any time in my busy schedule where I can crave you like I need to. I'm coaching this and that. I'm on every committee. Blah, blah, blah."

"What about your lunch break?" He asked.

"Well, God, that's only thirty minutes. And you know, that's when the guys and I usually go down to that special cafe that we like so much. You know, the one that has the great homemade pie and everything."

I kind of tossed that out as an excuse and didn't say anything else. But I knew that wasn't going to cut it. I knew that wasn't good enough. I knew how champions craved. I'd been a part of numerous championship teams. I knew what we did. I knew what it took to get there. We did *extra*—lots of it. And here I was, acting like I couldn't spare thirty minutes for God!

"That's it," I said. "I'm doing it. I'm giving Him my lunchtime. He told me to do it, and I'm doing it."

So the next day, I got up and made my bologna sandwich, grabbed some tapes, grabbed my Bible, and took off for work.

When I got there, I said, "Guys, I'm not going to be going with you to lunch anymore. Nothing against you. I like you and everything. But I just want to spend some time with God."

I was pumped! I wanted to be a champion for Him.

But then when lunchtime came, it wasn't quite what I expected it to be. I thought that I would receive all kinds of outstanding revelations, with sounds of a heavenly choir in the background singing "Hallelujah!" But that didn't happen. I plugged in a tape, followed along in my Bible, and ate my bologna sandwich. Period. It was actually kind of boring.

Because of that, I wasn't quite as excited the next day, but I did it anyway, because I was determined to crave God and be a champion.

The same thing happened.

Several days went by. No outstanding revelations. No choir. No "Hallelujah!"

After about a week, I found another fifteen minutes I could set aside for praise and worship. So I started giving that time to God as well as my lunchtime.

Then one day my boss called me and wanted to schedule a meeting during my praise and worship time.

I said, "Sir, I can't do it at that time."

"No," he told me, "that's the time we always do it."

"Sir, with all due respect to you as my boss, I can't do it at that time. I'll come in early in the morning. I'll stay after practice. I'll do anything you want me to do, but *please* don't take that time."

He asked me why.

"Don't ask me why. Just don't take that time."

"Okay," he said. "I'll call some people and see if we can change it."

When I hung up the phone, the Lord told me, "You're craving Me."

At that point in time, that craving literally overtook me, and I haven't been the same since.

It was like I had hit what is known as a "runner's high." After they've been running for a while, long-distance runners reach a place where their endorphins kick in. This simple release of chemicals in the body makes them feel so good that even though they've been running for a long time, they don't want to stop. Suddenly, there is no more fighting, no more struggling, no more fatigue. It seems like they could run forever.

You talk about a changed person! We'd be at a game somewhere and I was supposed to be handing out lineup cards at home plate before we got started. But I wouldn't be at home plate.

"Where's Coach Brim?" the other guys would ask each other.

I was out in the outfield praising God!

"God, I just want to thank You for this beautiful day and all these fans!"

I was *craving* Him! I wanted to be with Him as much as possible. Not for the rewards. Just because I loved Him.

By this time, nobody could take away my time with God. I even started looking for ways to find *more* time to be with Him. That craving for Him had overtaken me to the point that I didn't want to go anywhere or do anything without talking to Him first.

Even while I was coaching, I found about three hours in the day for worship and study time and never missed a beat in my schedule. I used my planning period for worship time. I stayed in my office and studied during my lunch break. And then when I got home in the evening, I found some extra time there instead of all the television I'd been watching.

I *craved* Him! Not because I wanted something from Him. I just wanted *Him*. I just wanted to spend time with Him because I loved Him and reverenced Him as my God. We were created to give Him glory and I wanted to do that in every way that I possibly could.

My life hasn't been the same since. I've gone to a whole new level in my relationship with the Lord.

And guess what? Because God can see my heart and knows I'm craving *Him* and not the blessings, He blesses me anyway, because that's just the way He is. He's a good God!

Isn't that what those verses said that we looked at earlier? When our hearts are right and we're diligently seeking Him, the blessings and rewards naturally follow us and begin to flood our lives.

CHAPTER 3

"Train Up Champions for Me"

One of the most amazing rewards of craving God was that He began to talk to me on a daily basis. He can do that if you're craving Him, because you're finally paying attention to Him, and He knows He won't be wasting His breath.

You see, we may want God to talk to us, but we're not ready to hear what He has to say. God may even have some big assignment for us, but we're not in the right position to fulfill it.

And God knows that. He's not stupid. So He'll just wait until we're serious about seeking Him. He'll wait until we begin craving Him. He'll wait until our ears are open and our hearts are ready to respond.

"It's Time"

One day while I was in my office seeking the Lord, I heard Him say, "It's time."

"Time for what?" I asked. "What are You talking about, Lord?"

"Time to preach," He replied.

"Oh, *that!*"

I knew exactly what He was talking about.

God blessed me as a coach because my heart was right toward Him, but He really hadn't called me to coach. He had called me to preach.

That call had come thirteen years earlier, back in 1986 at my dad's funeral.

Dad was only forty-nine years old when he died. I had just graduated from college, and I felt robbed.

Dad had been an honored athlete in football, baseball, and track and the two of us really connected on sports. He had always wanted to coach. That was his dream. But he never got around to it, because he had to work really hard all his life as a pipe fitter to provide for our family. He gave up his dream for us kids.

Well, I was going to give him his dream. I was going to have him help me coach. I was going to have him be right there with me.

But then he died. It was such a disappointment.

So we were all at the funeral, and I was sitting on the front row next to my mom. Brother Kenneth E. Hagin preached the service, and he was talking about "Finishing Your Race."

Next thing I knew, I was burning up.

I leaned over and elbowed Mom. "Mom," I whispered, "I'm burning! My hands, my ears, my face—they're all burning!"

I'd never felt anything like that before. It was so strong on me, I felt like I was going to explode!

At first I thought, *What is wrong with me? Somebody take me to the hospital!* But eventually I realized that it was the anointing, and then I just *knew* that Brother Hagin had a word from the Lord for me.

I told Mom, and I thought it was humorous that she said, "No, Honey, I think he has a word for me."

I thought, *What? You're not burning like me.*

Besides, I never, ever wanted a word before. I didn't like people, or I should say God, "reading my mail."

But this time I knew: This wasn't Mom's. This was mine.

I finally told Mom that I needed to stand up and interrupt Brother Hagin and tell him that he was missing God by continuing to preach. He needed to stop and tell me what it was God had given him to say to me.

Fortunately, I didn't do that. I came mighty close, though. I got as far as standing up and pointing my finger at him, but then I sat back down when he turned in my direction.

Sure enough, Brother Hagin *did* have a word from the Lord for me.

Right about then, he stopped his preaching and said, "What I'm about to do is prophesy, and it's a word from the Lord. And the one it is for, I'm sure, knows who it is for."

I *knew*, all right! It *had* to be me! There I was, burning up, weeping, and crying—I didn't know *what* was going on! The anointing of God was all over me in a way I had never experienced before.

Brother Hagin had been on the other side of the room, but now he came back over to where I was and said, "This is for Chipper." (He's about one of three people who can call me that and get away with it. That's because we have a relationship that goes way back to when I was a kid and my mom was working for him.)

He began to talk about how the anointing was now on me to finish the race. He said that my dad had been given a ministry, but he didn't fulfill it because of feelings of inadequacy.

Then he said, "If you will fulfill that ministry, you'll be blessed and your family will be blessed and people will call you blessed."

I knew it, I knew it, I knew it, I knew it, I knew it. I knew it before he even told me. But it was thirteen years before I responded to that call.

Why? Why the wait?

It was those same feelings of inadequacy that had kept my dad from finishing his race. I just wasn't sure I could do it.

As I said before, my dad was a pipe fitter. Mom was the preacher. But in spite of that, Dad was called out and prophesied over about the healing ministry the Lord had called him to in three different meetings by three different well-known men of God.

He had a strong healing anointing on him— and he knew it—but he let Satan intimidate him.

He'd say things to Mom like, "Who am I? I haven't been to Bible school. I don't even know half the verses you know, Honey. I probably don't even know ten. I don't know this stuff. Who would listen to me? Who could I lay hands on?"

It was just a bunch of low-level devils sent to harass him, and lie to him, and talk him out of the ministry God had called him to. Unfortunately, they succeeded.

Now those same low-level devils were harassing me. So when the Lord told me it was time to preach, I was reluctant to go along with Him.

"Lord," I began, "I'm just going to talk to You like You're here, because I know You *are* here. All I know how to do is coach. I couldn't preach. I don't know how to preach."

All of a sudden, my mind went back to my dad's funeral. After Brother Hagin had given me that word and the funeral was over, all kinds of people came up to me and told me that they would pay my way to Bible school.

My mom even got in on it. "Where are you going to Bible school? Do you want to go tomorrow?"

They all meant well, but it really put a lot of pressure on me.

Thank God for my pastor, Lee Morgans. He sensed what was happening and came over and said, "Chip, I don't care if they *all* come up. Seek God and do what *He* tells you to do."

So I sought the Lord about it—as much as I knew how then—but I didn't have a peace about going to Bible school. I pursued my coaching career instead.

But now, in light of what God was saying to me, I dropped to my knees in my office and started weeping.

"God, I missed it! I didn't go to Bible school. I've wasted thirteen years of my life!"

"No, you didn't," He told me. "Training champions was your Bible school. I need you to train champions for Me."

"But God, I don't know how to preach."

"Have I blessed you in coaching?" He asked.

"God, You've *blessed* me, and I've given glory to You in every game."

"I'll bless you to preach, too," He explained.

That got my attention and started me thinking: *Yeah, You could do that. I know You could do that!*

"Did I help you train up champions in the world?" He asked.

"Oh yes, God! When my guys leave here, they are *definitely* champions!"

"I'm coming back for a champion Church. Now I will help you train champions for Me."

It was an offer I couldn't refuse.

Unexpected Confirmation

So right there in the office, I committed and submitted myself to the will of God for my life.

I was so excited! I was jumping up and down, shouting, "Glory to God! Praise God! Champions for Christ!"

I had no idea what that meant. Here I'd just had a life-changing call from the Lord, and I didn't know what in the world to do with it.

I called Mom to tell her about it. She was on the other line with my sister Shelli.

"You've been called? Praise God! What did He say to you?"

"Champions for Christ."

We all started jumping up and down and shouting.

"Well, what is that?"

"I don't know."

"Well, Honey, that's okay," Mom told me. "Just keep seeking God."

I knew what that meant, so I started craving Him even more than I had been.

That went on for about two weeks. During that time, a number of people came up to me and said, "Hey, I heard you got the call to preach."

"Yeah, I'm going to preach," I'd tell them.

"What about?"

"Champions for Christ."

"What's that?"

"Well, I don't know."

Finally, God arranged a divine appointment for me with Brother Jerry Savelle that brought the picture into sharper focus.

I was attending a ministers' conference with my mom, and she called him over to speak with me after one of the sessions.

"Jerry, Jerry!" she called. "Come over here. My son has just changed his life."

Normally I would have felt extremely out of place talking with him, out of respect for him and his ministry. But this time was different. This time the grace of God was on me, and I shared with him out of my heart as if I'd known him all my life.

"Jerry," I said, "God talked to me about training up champions for Him—champions for Christ."

Jerry got excited. "Praise God! Did you say champions for Christ? One time He told me about training up champions, too!"

Then Jerry went on with this great story about how God had used him in this area.

Back in the early days of Jerry's ministry, God opened up doors for him to speak to the San Francisco Forty-Niners. This was back when Joe Montana was their quarterback, and they were back-to-back world champions. It was an awesome opportunity!

43

So Jerry was all excited and was just thanking God for opening those doors. "Thank You, God! What do You want me to tell them? What do You want me to preach on? O Lord, just give it to me! I'll tell them. I'll tell them whatever You say."

Then the Lord said, "Jerry, I want you to tell them how to be champions."

"Say what?" Jerry asked in disbelief.

"I want you to tell them how to be champions."

Jerry couldn't believe his ears.

"Lord," he objected, "I don't know if You're aware of this or not, but we're talking about the San Francisco Forty-Niners here. They're all wearing two Super Bowl rings that say 'World Champions'—and You want *me* to teach *them* to be champions?"

"Yes, they're champion football players," the Lord answered him, "but they're not champion husbands. They're not champion fathers. They're not living like champions at home."

That's when Jerry saw it. He saw exactly what God was talking about. So that's what he shared when he went to talk to the San Francisco Forty-Niners.

Jerry told me that when he began to speak to the players, the presence of God fell. Many were touched by God.

Jerry said that some of them came up to him, tears streaming down their faces, saying things like, "I'm going to stop cheating on my wife when I'm on the road." "I'm going to be a better husband." "I'm going to be a better father to my children."

You see, God knew just what they needed, and it wasn't another Super Bowl ring. They already knew how to be champions on the field. They needed to know how to be champions in their daily lives.

God was much more interested in their being champion husbands and fathers than in their being champion football players. Yes, God wants us to be champions at our jobs. But that's only part of the story. He wants us to be champions in every area of our lives.

After hearing this story of Jerry's, I began to get a clearer picture of what God wanted me to do. I began to see that training champions for Him is not about winning some kind of trophy. It's not about receiving the MVC Award—Most Valuable Christian—in some kind of spiritual showdown with fellow believers. It's not about competing with other churches or ministries.

Training champions for Christ is about helping people win in life. It's about helping them be champion husbands and wives. It's about helping them be champion fathers and mothers. It's about helping them be champion sons and daughters. It's about helping them be successful and healthy and prosperous in the natural realm as well as successful and healthy and prosperous in the spiritual realm. It's about helping them be successful in their walk with God and successful in enforcing Jesus' defeat over the devil. It's all of that and more.

Now *that* was something I could get excited about! I could hardly wait to get started!

CHAPTER 4

Strong and Mighty Warriors

"Okay, Lord. I see what You mean now about training up champions for You. You're coming back soon, and You want to see a glorious Church—a Church full of champions."

I was pumped! I thought, *This is going to be great!*

So I started studying on champions in the Bible, but it wasn't quite what I expected. Has that ever happened to you? You get something from God, but then you start studying it, and it turns out to be nothing like you thought it would be.

That's what happened in this case. When I looked up the word *champion* in the Bible, I found out that it was there only three times—and it was all about Goliath.

I was kind of disappointed. "Lord, I know there's got to be something here about champions, and I know it's not about Goliath, that headless dude. He lost!"

"It's all throughout the Bible," He told me.

"No, I looked it up," I insisted. "It's only in there three times."

But He just kept assuring me that champions were found throughout the Bible.

So I decided to keep studying. This time, instead of just looking up the verses where the word *champion* was used, I decided to look up the word itself. That's when things got interesting.

I found out that in Hebrew, the word for *champion* is *gibbor*. It means "strong," "a mighty man," "a valiant man."

Now we're talking! I thought.

Then I decided to check out the Hebrew root word for *champion*. (In Hebrew, all of the words come from root words. Each root word has a number of related words branching out from it, like spokes branching out from the hub of a wagon wheel. And each of these related words carries something of the meaning of the root word.)

I found that *champion* comes from the root word *gavar*. Talk about a loaded word! It means "to be strong," "to prevail," "to be great," "to be mighty," "to be valiant," "to be courageous." Wow!

In other words, a champion is a strong and mighty warrior, one who prevails.

I remembered that Abraham's faith was strong. In other words, he had champion (fully persuaded) faith.

I was also reminded of what Paul said in Ephesians, "Be strong in the Lord." He was saying, "Be a champion."

So I shifted gears and started looking up the words *strong* and *mighty* in the Scriptures. Sure enough—they were found all throughout the Bible, just like the Lord told me.

In both the Old and New Testaments, God commanded His people to be champions. In other words, it is not just a privilege to be a champion—it is an obligation, an order!

Then I saw it. That's it! That's us! That's what God wants us to be. Champions—strong and mighty warriors who always prevail!

Anointed To Win

Immediately God started showing me other important things about champions. One of them was in 1 Samuel 16, where Samuel anoints David to be king.

Then Samuel took the horn of oil, and anointed David in the midst of his brothers; and **the Spirit of the Lord came mightily upon David from that day forward**.

1 SAMUEL 16:13 (AMP)

"Lord, do you mean that the Spirit came on him like a champion?" I asked.

"Yes," He answered.

Then I began to see how that related to us as believers today.

When we're born again, the Spirit of the Lord—the spirit of *the* Champion—begins to reside in us. As far as God is concerned, we're champions right then, from that moment forward. We're strong in His might, and we possess everything we need to prevail over the devil in every situation. That's a spiritual reality.

God desires for things on earth to be as they are in heaven. Jesus mentioned this when He taught the disciples about prayer.

Thy kingdom come. Thy will be done in earth, as it is in heaven.

MATTHEW 6:10

Since we know that Jesus wouldn't have prayed something that wasn't the will of God, we can be sure this is how God the Father feels about the matter, too.

And how are things in heaven? Awesome! Streets of gold. Mansions. No poverty. No need. No lack. No want. No sickness. No worry. No sorrow. No pain. Just abundant life.

Jesus also made it clear that this abundant life isn't only for when we get to heaven. He said He came so that we could start living that abundant life *now*.

> The thief comes only in order that he may steal and may kill and may destroy. I came that they may have and enjoy life, and have it in abundance—to the full, till it overflows.
>
> JOHN 10:10 (AMP)

This is the will of God for you. This is the will of God for me. This is the will of God for every believer. To have heaven on earth. To have abundant life.

That's what being a champion is all about: living the abundant life.

The Bible tells us in 2 Corinthians 5:20 that we're Christ's ambassadors, His representatives. In other words, we're supposed to look and act like Him—and He's a champion!

He doesn't want us to be a bunch of weak, shy, ashamed, embarrassed, fearful, beggarly wimps. He wants us to be bold, strong, fearless, mighty champions! He wants us to walk in His champion anointing!

When?

Right now. There's no more time to waste. We can't wait anymore. Time is running out. Jesus is coming back soon. We need to be living like champions *now*—for our own sakes and for the sake of other people.

Be a Warrior

Abundant life isn't something we earn. It's a gift. Jesus already bought and paid for it with His blood.

But if we want to *walk* in that abundant life—if we want to *live* like a champion—we're going to have to work at it. It's going to require some effort on our part.

Think about it for a moment. We said that champions were strong and mighty warriors, ones who prevail. The very definition itself suggests a struggle or battle. It implies that there is something or someone we are warring against. You can't prevail unless there is something or someone to prevail *over*.

So what are we warring against? Over whom are we supposed to be prevailing?

The devil and his works.

He's our enemy, and we can count on him to put up some resistance. He's the thief that Jesus talked about in John 10:10, and he has only one thing on his mind: to try to steal, kill, and destroy what God has made available to us. He's going to do everything he can to try to keep us from living like champions.

The good news is that we don't have to settle for Satan's plan! Jesus already took care of that for us.

> Behold! I have given **you** authority and power to trample upon serpents and scorpions, and (physical and mental strength and ability) over all the power that the enemy [possesses], and nothing shall in any way harm you.
>
> LUKE 10:19 (AMP)

> For though we walk [live] in the flesh, **we** are not carrying on our warfare according to the flesh and using mere human weapons. For the weapons of **our** warfare are not physical (weapons of flesh and blood), but they are mighty before God for the overthrow and destruction of strongholds.
>
> 2 CORINTHIANS 10:3-4 (AMP)

Jesus defeated Satan and has given us everything we need to be able to live in victory over him. Praise God!

Look at those verses again. There's something else we need to see here.

God has already done His part. He's already won the victory and defeated the devil for us. But now *we* have to *enforce* that defeat by refusing to let the devil rob us of what God has given us.

Notice the words *you, we,* and *our* in those verses. It's clear that God has given us the power and ability to prevail every time we face the devil, but it's also clear that *we* have to *do* something with that power and ability. We have to make *use* of what God has given us if we're going to live in victory.

Think about the story of David and Goliath. Because the Israelites had a covenant with God, they had a champion's anointing on them. They could have defeated Goliath any time. But instead of drawing on that anointing and prevailing over their enemy, they let themselves be intimidated by him. Instead of going after him and enforcing his defeat, they backed off in doubt and fear and cowered in their tents.

Not David. He *knew* he had that champion's anointing on him. But that wasn't all. He *did* something with it. He went and picked out those stones and took off after the enemy. You know the rest of the story—bye-bye, Goliath!

David knew his covenant rights. Champions know their covenant rights. That's why David said to Goliath, "You uncircumcised Philistine." In other words, you don't have a covenant with the Almighty God, and I do; therefore you can never win, and I will always win.

There is a covenant agreement between two parties—God and us. Our part: obedience, faith, love. God's part: to make sure we *always* triumph in Christ Jesus.

Always! So if you are going through a test or trial—good news! It's not over until you win!

It was the will of God for Goliath and the Philistines to be defeated. And God supplied all the power necessary for that to happen. But before His will could actually be seen and experienced in the earth, somebody had to hook up with Him in faith and walk it out.

The same is true for us today.

God has made us champions. He's given us all the power and equipment we need. That is His part.

Now it's time for our part. It's time for us to lay hold of those things in faith and make a quality decision that we are *not* going to give up, give in, or be backed off of the promises and blessings of God—ever! No matter what comes our way. No matter how tough it gets.

We're champions! We're strong and mighty warriors! We *always* prevail!

It's time we started acting like it. God never meant for these truths to be just words on a page. He wants us to *live* it!

One time after I preached this message about being champions for Christ, a woman ran up to me after the service. Tears were running down her face as she hugged me and said, "I'm a missionary to Russia. We just had a revival among the youth there, and the message was on being champions for the Lord!"

Hallelujah! God is getting this message out all over the world in all kinds of ways. He's highlighting it. He wants us to get it and He wants us to start living it—now! Not in a few years when we get around to it. Now. Right now.

So what are we waiting for? Let's do it!

CHAPTER 5

Championship Living

There's an old saying that it takes a champion to train a champion.

I believe that. A loser can't train a champion, because he's never been there. He doesn't know what it takes to get there.

With that in mind, it's encouraging for us as believers to know that we have the best possible Trainer—the Lord—and He is definitely a Champion!

> Who is this King of glory? The Lord **strong and mighty**, the Lord **mighty in battle**.
>
> PSALM 24:8

Praise God, we're in good hands! The greatest Champion ever is on our side, and He's going to teach us everything we need to know.

He needs us now for these last days, and He's going to get us ready.

Incidentally, this principle of champions training champions is a message for parents, too. (I'm a parent, so I include myself in this.) As the Lord trains us to be champions, we are to pass that training along to our children and raise them to be champions.

An interesting verse related to this is found in the Book of Psalms.

> As arrows are in the hand of a **mighty** man; so are children of the youth.
> PSALM 127:4

Let's look at that for a moment. It says that children are to be like arrows in the hand of a champion.

I love to bow hunt. (One reason is that sitting up in a deer stand at 4:30 in the morning is a great prayer closet! It's just you, God, and all of creation. It's awesome!)

But there's some skill required in shooting a bow and arrow. It takes training and practice to develop the necessary accuracy. You have to be taught. Unless you learn how to aim and guide those arrows properly, they're liable to fly off in all directions. No telling where they'll end up. You might never find them again.

God doesn't want that to happen to our children. He wants them to be aimed in the right direction. He wants us to teach them to be champions.

In Hebrew, the word for *teach* means "to shoot straight." God wants us to guide our children so they will hit the mark, and live like champions.

Champions training champions. The Lord trains us, and then we train others. That's what it's all about.

Of course, we never really get through learning. We never arrive at the point where we know everything, but we can share what we *do* know. We can pass along what we *have* learned. That's what I want to do in the next few pages: I want to share some of what God has shown me about being a champion.

Keep Your Priorities Straight

One of the basic things the Lord taught me about being a champion is that champions are focused. They're disciplined. They eliminate distractions that can drain them of time, energy, and resources and keep them from reaching their goal.

In other words, champions keep their priorities straight. The championship comes first.

I applied this priority-setting principle with my players when I was coaching. When practice was over, I'd tell them, "Guys, I can't teach you everything you need to know about being a champion in a few hours of practice a week. It's just not going to happen. If you want a college or professional team to come here and sign you, you're going to have to practice some personal discipline. You're going to have to keep your priorities straight. When you have free time, you're going to have to forget about girls, forget about dragging Main Street, and forget about playing Nintendo. You're going to have to get yourself back out to this field, and you're going to have to practice. That's the only way it's going to happen."

That wasn't just a pep talk. That was the truth. And I meant every word of it.

We faced teams all the time that didn't have any discipline. Sloppy. Late. Too much horsing around. And I can tell you this: Those teams were *never* championship teams. My guys could tell just by looking at them that we were going to beat them.

Why?

Because we were disciplined, and they weren't. It's just that simple.

You'll never see a championship team that isn't disciplined. Other teams may have greater athletes. Other teams may have greater talent. But if they don't have discipline, they'll lose it at the finish line. They won't have what it takes to win.

God wants us to win. He wants us to complete our race. He wants us to cross the finish line.

But that only comes by discipline. That only comes by having right priorities. That only comes by putting Him first. Every day. All the time.

Christians often refer to themselves as *disciples* of Christ. The word *disciple* comes from the word *discipline*. In other words, a disciple is "a disciplined one."

It's time for us to be real disciples of Christ. It's time for us to be disciplined ones in our walk with Him.

Start craving Him. Start looking for ways to rearrange your schedule to make time for Him. Start turning off the television once in awhile and spend that time with Him instead. Quit watching those movies and reading those magazines that pull your heart away from Him. Start putting Him first.

Instead of reaching a runner's high, you will reach the craver's high. And that's where you won't let anyone or anything take your time with God

I promise you, it will change your life! He'll talk to you. He'll use you. He'll bless you.

That's certainly been true in my own life. When I started putting God first—I mean *really* putting Him first—things changed dramatically for me. And now I'd have to say that training champions for Christ is far more satisfying than any honor I ever received in my coaching career. After all, we're not just talking about winning a state championship here. We're talking about pleasing God and obtaining *eternal* rewards! What can possibly compare with that?

Dress Like a Champion

Another thing about champions is that they look like champions. They dress like it.

I remember when we finally won our first championship. The next year we bought the best uniforms money could buy. No raggedy old threads for us. No spots or wrinkles. No way!

When we stepped off that bus and ran onto the field—wow! We were champions, and everybody knew it. It intimidated the other team just to look at us. Even the way we were dressed said, "We're champions! And you'd better get ready, because we're here to beat you! We're going to win!"

We've got a special uniform in the Church. It's called the armor of God, and we see it mentioned several places in the New Testament.

> The night is far spent, the day is at hand: let us therefore cast off the works of darkness, and let us put on the **armour** of light.
>
> ROMANS 13:12

> By the word of truth, by the power of God, by the **armour** or righteousness on the right hand and on the left.
>
> 2 CORINTHIANS 6:7

> Put on the whole **armour** of God, that ye may be able to stand against the wiles of the devil. For we wrestle not against flesh and blood, but against principalities, against powers, against the rulers of the darkness of this world, against spiritual wickedness in high places. Wherefore take

unto you the whole **armour** of God, that ye may be able to withstand in the evil day, and having done all, to stand. Stand therefore, having your loins girt about with truth, and having on the breastplate of righteousness; And your feet shod with the preparation of the gospel of peace; Above all, taking the shield of faith, wherewith ye shall be able to quench all the fiery darts of the wicked. And take the helmet of salvation, and the sword of the Spirit, which is the word of God: Praying always with all prayer and supplication in the Spirit, and watching thereunto with all perseverance and supplication for all saints.

EPHESIANS 6:11-18

Usually, we think of armor as protection. Something defensive. But if we look up the word *armor* as it is used in these verses, we find that it is *offensive* as well.

That's important. We have to learn to use our armor defensively *and* offensively.

In all my years of coaching, we never won a single baseball game simply by keeping the other team from scoring. That helped, of course, and it was important to play good defense. But we couldn't win the game unless *we* put some runs on the board. If *we* didn't score, the best we could come up with was a tie.

God is not interested in us coming out in a tie or being defeated by the devil. He wants us to win!

That means we're going to have to stop putting all our efforts into defense and start playing some offense. We're going to have to start making full use of our armor. The devil has been harassing the Church for way too long. It's time we started harassing him!

Championship teams put pressure on the opposition. Champions are always on the move and in your face. You never know what they're going to do next. They constantly bring the game to you and do everything they can to force errors on your part.

On my teams, for example, I always had the guys attempt to steal second base whenever they made it to first. I didn't care if they could run or not. I didn't even care that the other team knew we were going to do it.

Why?

Because we wanted to keep the pressure on them. They were going to have to do five or six things right before they could get us out on that play. The pitcher was going to have to throw a good pitch. The catcher was going to have to catch it, not just block it in the dirt. Then he was going to have to throw it on target. Then the shortstop or second baseman was going to have to catch it. Then they were going to have to make the tag without dropping the ball.

See what I mean? And we didn't do that just once. We did it *all day long!*

Eventually, you could see the pressure affecting the other team, wearing them down. Every time the pitcher would walk somebody, you could almost hear the catcher thinking, *Oh, man! Quit walking them! You know he's going to run!*

That's how we played every game—all out. We kept the pressure on them. We called the shots and made them play *our* game. And that pressure eventually forced them to make mistakes.

Not everybody played that way, though. A lot of teams had more of a defensive mind-set and chose to play it safe. If they didn't think their guys were very fast, they wouldn't attempt to steal. If they didn't think their guys could pull off a bunt, they wouldn't give it a try. As a result, they were never a threat to their opponents. And they were never champions.

The Church has been far too passive. The devil comes, slaps us around a little, and we just sit there and take it.

"Well, that wasn't too bad," we rationalize. "I can live with it."

I know. I did that all my life.

Forget that stuff! God doesn't want us to "live with" anything from the devil!

You're a champion! Your days of settling for the devil's plan for your life are over!

It's time we started putting some pressure on the opposon. "Look out, devil! Here we come! Right here! Right now!"

Once when I was preaching this message, God gave an eleven-year-old Native American boy a special revelation. It affected him so much that he even came up before the congregation of hundreds of people to share what had happened to him. (I can tell you from personal experience, that's unusual. I was raised by a Native American, and they tend to be *very* quiet. The boy's dad came up to me afterwards, saying how touching this was, because his son usually never said anything.)

Here's what happened: At one point in the service, I said, "All right, if you're a champion, stand up!" Then while we were all standing there, God allowed this boy to see into the spirit realm.

The boy later told his dad that everyone had their armor on. And some of them, not everyone, had their swords drawn. "Dad, the armor was glowing," he said, "and then the trumpet was blown and it stopped."

I began to wonder about that, so I asked the Lord about it.

"Lord, what about the swords? Why did some of the people have them drawn and some of them didn't?"

He showed me that the ones holding up their swords were the ones who were on offense. They were using their armor for its intended purpose—defensively *and* offensively.

And what about the glowing? What was that?

Remember Romans 13:12? It refers to the armor of *light*.

God is pure light, and His light overpowers and drives away darkness. And now that we're born again, we have that same light of God dwelling in us. That's what Paul was talking about in Ephesians 5:8 when he said that now we are "light in the Lord," and we are to walk as "children of light." That light of God is what makes us glow in the spirit realm.

And the trumpet?

In the old days, just before an army got ready to advance, they blew a trumpet. After that, the leader would yell, "CHARGE!" and the troops would take out after the enemy. Not only did that trumpet sound rally the troops, but it was a bold statement to the enemy that they were coming after them.

God showed all of this to that little boy to help us, because we need to get a grip on this. This is spiritual reality. This is how God sees us and it's time we started seeing ourselves that same way.

Don't wait for a problem to show up before you grab your Bible. We saw earlier in Ephesians 6:17 that the Word of God is the sword of the Spirit. Keep your sword drawn. Think offensively, not just defensively. Stay full of the Word all the time, continually speaking it over yourself and your family.

The devil can't stand that. He doesn't have any defense against the Word. So go ahead and let him have it! Blow your trumpet, sound that charge, and let him know you're coming after him with all the power of God behind you!

CHAPTER 6

Never Let 'Em See You Sweat

One final thing about champions: They never let the opposition see them sweat. Even if they are tempted to feel scared, or nervous, or to think about quitting, champions never—*never*—give *any* kind of sign to their opponents that they feel that way.

We used to love it when the opposing team would start kicking the dirt. We'd start jumping and shouting and high-fiving each other, because we knew that meant they had lost their confidence. They'd lost their focus. And we knew we had them then.

Fear and weakness are like magnets to the devil. He's on that in a heartbeat. So even if we slip up or come under attack at some point, we need to just make any necessary adjustments and keep on going forward without batting an eye.

I always told my pitchers, "Don't *ever* let me see you kicking the dirt! I don't care if they hit the farthest home run in baseball history. You get another ball from the catcher, and get right back up there on the pitcher's mound, just like nothing happened. Act more confident than you ever have before. Don't give up. Think like a champion. Keep your eyes on the goal!"

According to Philippians 1:28, that's how we're to handle the devil as believers.

> And do not [for a moment] be frightened or intimidated in anything by your opponents and adversaries, for such [constancy and fearlessness] will be a clear sign (proof and seal) to them of [their impending] destruction; but [a sure token and evidence] of your deliverance and salvation, and that from God.
>
> PHILIPPIANS 1:28 (AMP)

The devil can't read your mind; he has to have a sign. The signs are fear and intimidation.

The fact that we're not moved by anything the devil does is a sure sign to him that he's in trouble.

Think of it this way. Let's say I was at the mall with my wife. Some big ol' guy comes up and grabs her purse, so I take off after him. When I catch up to him, he turns around and hits me with the hardest punch he's got. I take it on the chin, but then I just look at him with a big smile on my face.

What's he going to be thinking?

Uh-oh! I'm in trouble now! I gave him my best shot, and it didn't even faze him!

That's what we're talking about. We set our face like flint, and we *never* let the devil see us sweat. No matter what he says, no matter what he does, we remain constant, steadfast, and fearless.

Don't waste time talking about how the devil is harassing you, or about what he's trying to do in your life. Don't glorify him in any way, or give him any more thought than is absolutely necessary. Do what you have to do to deal with him, then move on. He's not worth it.

If you want someone to agree with you in prayer, or you want to go up in a ministry line during a service, that's fine. But do those things in faith, not fear. It's only a tip-off to the devil if you're not in faith. So don't go there whining, worrying, and begging God to help you. Go there in faith and confidence, knowing that you've got the victory, and you're going to receive everything that you need from the Lord.

A Champion's Confession

We *are* champions! God made us that way. It's time for us to start <u>talking</u> like it. It's time for us to start <u>looking</u> like it. It's time for us to start <u>acting</u> like it. Everywhere. All the time.

If you'd like to join me in being a champion for Christ, I encourage you to make this your confession:

- In Christ
- I'm strong!
- I'm mighty!
- I'm a warrior!
- I've got on the armor of light, and
- I'm ready for battle!
- Do you hear that trumpet, devil?
- That means I'm going on offense and
- I'm coming after you!
- And I *will* prevail, because
- I'M A CHAMPION FOR CHRIST!

A Prayer of Salvation

If you have never met Jesus Christ, you can know Him today. God cares for you and wants to help you in every area of your life. That is why He sent Jesus to die for you. You can make your life right with God this very moment and make heaven your home.

Pray this prayer now:

Oh, God, I ask You to forgive me of my sins. I believe You sent Jesus to die on the cross for me. I receive Jesus Christ as my personal Lord and Savior. I confess Him as Lord of my life, and I give my life to Him. Thank You, Lord, for saving me and for making me new. In Jesus' name, amen.

If you just prayed this prayer, I welcome you to the family of God. The angels in heaven are rejoicing with you right now.

I prayed this prayer today:

Name_____

Date_____

ABOUT THE AUTHOR

In 1998, Chip Brim left a successful baseball career to fulfill the call of the ministry. "It's time!" the Lord said to him. "I have taught you to train champions in baseball. Now it's time to train Champions for Christ."

Through a supernatural experience, God gave Chip a message that explains why Christians are not receiving the answers to their prayers.

Chip is a powerful speaker, preaching all over the United States, where the Holy Spirit endorses his ministry with salvations, healings, and deliverances.

Chip, his wife, Candace, and their two children reside near Branson, Missouri.

For information about products by Chip Brim, or ministry and scheduling information, write:

Champions 4 Christ
c/o Billye Brim Ministries
P.O. Box 40
Branson, MO 65615

Phone: (417) 336-4877

or visit our Web site:
www.champions4christ.org

ATTENTION CHAMPIONS!

Inspired by and in honor of *The Champion*, Chip Brim has commissioned a *Champions 4 Christ* championship ring. This beautiful ring is a great witnessing tool and an awesome reminder of who you are in Christ.

For pricing and ordering information, please write: